Unbelievable Pictures and Facts About Belgium

By: Olivia Greenwood

Introduction

Belgium is a beautiful country. Here you will find many medieval towns and very old architecture. Today we will be exploring the country of Belgium in more detail. We hope you learn some interesting stuff.

Do many people come to visit Belgium?

Over the years Belgium has become a very popular country for people to visit. There are millions of people who come to visit Belgium each and every single year.

Are there any rivers in Belgium?

There are many rivers in Belgium. The one which has gained the most attention is a river called Scheldt River. This river is the longest river in Belgium.

Which language do they speak the most in Belgium?

There are actually three languages which they speak the most in Belgium. These languages are Dutch, French and German.

Are there many museums to visit in Belgium?

If you enjoy visiting museums, you will really enjoy Belgium. The country is filled with all sorts of fascinating museums.

Are the men in Belgium tall or short?

The men in Belgium are known for being very tall. They are the second tallest men in the entire world.

Which sport is the most loved in the area?

The sport which people follow and love the most is none other than the popular sport football.

What items are exported the most?

Belgium is known for exporting many things. Some of the goods include cars, diamonds, and even petrol.

Which religion do they practice the most in the area?

The religion which is practiced the most in the area is Christianity. The majority of people in Belgium consider themselves to be Roman Catholic.

What types of food do they eat in Belgium?

The most popular type of food which is eaten in Belgium is seafood. They eat lots of seafood in the country.

Does Belgium have a national flower?

Belgium does have a national flower. The name of this national flower is the red poppy. Many years ago they would use this flower in herbal medicines to treat all sorts of ailments and diseases.

What is Belgium most well-known for?

Do you enjoy eating chocolate? Belgium is known throughout the world for its amazing chocolate.

Which financial currency do they make use of in Belgium?

Belgium makes use of the same currency as the rest of Europe. Can you guess what currency this is? If you guessed the Euro you guessed correctly.

What is the population size of Belgium?

The population of Belgium is growing each and every single day when a baby is born. On average there are currently over 11.54 million people living in Belgium.

Does Belgium hold a world record for anything?

The answer is a big yes. Belgium has a world record for something quite different and unusual. It has the record for the country going for the longest period of time without its own government.

Where is the tallest point in Belgium?

Far away in Haute Ardenne Mountain Rage, you will find the tallest point in Belgium. Signal de Botrange is known as the highest point in the whole of Belgium.

Does it cost a lot of money to visit Belgium?

Unfortunately, it does cost a lot of money to visit Belgium. Believe it or not, Belgium is one of the most expensive countries to visit in the entire world.

What type of weather does Belgium experience?

The climate in Belgium is usually very moderate and consistent. The weather temperatures seem to be just right.

It is safe to travel in Belgium?

The good news is that it is safe to travel in Belgium. However, just like anywhere else in the world, it is important to prioritize your safety and security at all times.

What type of landscape does Belgium have?

The country is surrounded by all sorts of landscape. Here you will find rocks, mountains, rivers, and even hills.

Where exactly is Belgium situated?

Belgium can be found far away in Western Europe. It can be found along a coastline very closely situated to the North Sea.

Made in the USA
Coppell, TX
01 March 2023